PREFACE

Many Christians think that Christianity and Islam are almost same. They even believe that Islam has it's root in Christianity. The main purpose of this book is to wipeout these misunderstanding. We expose Islam by revealing the major differences from Christianity. We pray that all of us to realize the truth about Islam and stand for our holy faith in our Lord and God Jesus Christ.

> "But even if we or an angel from heaven should preach a gospel other than the one we preached to you, let them be under God's curse! As we have already said, so now I say again: If anybody is preaching to you a gospel other than what you accepted, let them be under God's curse!"
>
> - Galatians 1:8,9

GOD OF BIBLE VS GOD OF QURAN

In the Bible, God is a Trinity

Father, Son, and Holy Spirit.

Isaiah 43:10; 44:6-8 | Matt. 28:19 | John 10:30 | 2 Cor. 13:14 | Hebrews 1:8

In Quran, God is not a Trinity

Surah 5:73, "They do blaspheme who say: Allah is one of three in a Trinity: for there is no god except One Allah. If they desist not from their word (of blasphemy), verily a grievous penalty will befall the blasphemers among them."

Because Islam denies the Trinity, in Islam, Jesus is not the incarnation of the second person of the Trinity

In the opening chapters of Genesis, we read of how God was to be found walking and talking in the garden with Adam and Eve. God walks and talks with Abraham (Genesis 17–18), speaks to Moses face to face 'as a man speaks with his friend' (Exodus 33:11), and, indeed God speaks with his people throughout the Old Testament.

And at the close of the Bible, we are promised that in the age to come -

And I heard a loud voice from the throne saying, "Look! God's dwelling place is now among the people, and he will dwell with them. They will be his people, and God himself will be with them and be their God.

- Revelation 21:3

According to the Qur'an, Allah did not walk and talk in the garden with Adam and Eve. He is not present with his people in heaven. The only 'relationship' that exists between humans and Allah according to the Qur'an is that of master and servant – not father or friend.

"Muslims do not see God as their father … Men are servants of a just master; they cannot, in orthodox Islam, typically attain any greater degree of intimacy with their creator."   - Shabbir Akhtar, A Faith for All Seasons (Chicago: Ivan R. Dee, 1990) 180

God loves the entire world

"But God demonstrates His own love toward us, in that while we were yet sinners, Christ died for us."   -Romans 5:8

God sent Jesus to die while we were still in our sins. He not only said He loved the whole world, but showed that He loved the world (Jn. 3:16).

Allah only loves Muslims

Allah does not love sinners. Surah 3:31-32 states that Allah does not love those who reject faith (or Islam), and in 3:57 it states that he does not love those who do wrong.

"Say: Obey Allah and the Messenger; but if they turn back, then surely Allah does not love the unbelievers," - Surahs 3:32
"...Allah is an enemy to those who reject Faith," - Surah 2:98

God is our Father not only in that he is our Creator but that he is also our Redeemer; this is what distinguishes the Christian's relationship to God and what allows us to relate to him as Father.

"You are our Father, though Abraham does not know us and Israel does not acknowledge us; you, O Lord, are our Father, our Redeemer from old is your name" - Isa. 63:16–17
"Because you are sons, God has sent the Spirit of his Son into our hearts, crying "Abba, Father!" So you are no longer a slave, but a son, and if a son, then an heir through God" - Gal. 4:6–7

"He is the Originator of the heavens and the earth. How can He have children when He has no wife? He created all things and He is the All-Knower of everything." - Surah 6:101

JESUS CHRIST VS ISA (MUSLIM JESUS)

Jesus is God in flesh

"For in Him all the fullness of Deity dwells in bodily form.." - Colossians 2:9

"In the beginning was the Word, and the Word was with God, and the Word was God" - John 1:1

"And the Word became flesh, and dwelt among us, and we saw His glory, glory as of the only begotten from the Father, full of grace and truth" - John 1:14

Isa is not God

"Indeed those who said: 'Christ, the son of Mary, he is indeed God', disbelieved." - Surah 5:17

"The Messiah, son of Mary, was no more than a Messenger before whom many Messengers have passed away.." - Surah 5:75

Jesus is the Son of God

"The beginning of the gospel of Jesus Christ, the Son of God" - Mark 1:1

Isa is not the Son of God

"...the Christians say, 'The Messiah is the son of Allah' That is their statement from their mouths; ...May Allah destroy them; how are they deluded?"   - Surah 5:17

Jesus was crucified

"When they came to the place called the Skull, they crucified him there, along with the criminals - one on his right, the other on his left"   - Luke 23:33

Isa was not crucified

"And for their saying, 'We have killed the Messiah, Jesus, the son of Mary, the Messenger of God.' In fact, they did not kill him, nor did they crucify him, but it appeared to them as if they did."   - Surah 4:157

Jesus rose from the dead

"The angel said to the women, "Do not be afraid, for I know that you are looking for Jesus, who was crucified. He is not here; he has risen, just as he said. Come and see the place where he lay."   - Matthew 28:5,6

Isa can't rose from the dead

As we saw that Isa of Quran was not crucified, he can't rose from the dead. It is absolutely opposite to the account of Jesus Christ which is written in the Holy Bible. **Hence, Isa of Quran is not the one and only savior and God - Jesus Christ.**

THE HOLY BIBLE VS THE QURAN

Here are some major differences in the teachings of Bible and Quran

Salvation by grace through faith

"For by grace you have been saved through faith; and that not of yourselves, it is the gift of God; not as a result of works, so that no one may boast."   - Ephesians 2:8-9

"That if you confess with your mouth, "Jesus is Lord," and believe in your heart that God raised him from the dead, you will be saved. For it is with your heart that you believe and are justified, and it is with your mouth that you confess and are saved."

                     - Romans 10:9-10

"O you who believe! If you are careful of (your duty to) Allah, He will grant you a distinction and do away with your evils and forgive you; and Allah is the Lord of mighty grace,"   - Surah 8:29
"Then those whose balance (of good deeds) is heavy, they will be successful. But those whose balance is light, will be those who have lost their souls; in hell will they abide,"
                            - Surah 23:102-103)

"You have heard that it was said, 'Love your neighbor[a] and hate your enemy.' But I tell you, love your enemies and pray for those who persecute you, that you may be children of your Father in heaven. He causes his sun to rise on the evil and the good, and sends rain on the righteous and the unrighteous."
                            - Matthew 5:43-48
"Do not repay evil with evil or insult with insult. On the contrary, repay evil with blessing, because to this you were called so that you may inherit a blessing." - 1 Peter 3:9

"The only reward of those who make war upon Allah and His messenger and strive after corruption in the land will be that they will be killed or crucified, or have their hands and feet on alternate sides cut off, or will be expelled out of the land. Such will be their degradation in the world, and in the Hereafter,"   - Surah 5:33

"Then, when the sacred months have passed, slay the idolaters wherever ye find them, and take them (captive), and besiege them, and prepare for them each ambush. But if they repent and establish worship and pay the poor-due, then leave their way free. Lo! Allah is Forgiving, Merciful,"   - Surah 9:5

"Now when ye meet in battle those who disbelieve, then it is smiting of the necks until, when ye have routed them, then making fast of bonds; and afterward either grace or ransom till the war lay down its burdens..."   - Surah 47:4

Heaven - where God, His holy angels, and His believing children dwell

Heaven is the place of the everlasting blessedness of the righteous; the abode of departed souls whose names are written in The Lamb's Book of Life. The blessings of heaven consist of the following

Eternal life

"Many of those who sleep in the dust of the ground will awake, these to everlasting life, but the others to disgrace and everlasting contempt."
- Daniel 12:2

"These will go away into eternal punishment, but the righteous into eternal life."
- Matthew 25:46

Eternal glory

"For our light affliction, which is but for a moment, worketh for us a far more exceeding and eternal weight of glory.."
- 2 Corinthians 4:17

Eternal bodies

"For we know that if our earthly house [physical body], this tent, is destroyed, we have a building from God, a house not made with hands, eternal in the heavens. For in this we groan, earnestly desiring to be clothed with our habitation which is from heaven.."
                              - 2 Corinthians 5:1-2

Rewards for the believers

"Rejoice and be glad, for your reward is great in heaven, for so men persecuted the prophets who were before you"
                              - Matthew 5:12

Reigning with Christ

"If we endure, we will also reign with him.."
                              - 2 Timothy 2:11

Live happy forever

"And God shall wipe away all tears from their eyes; and there shall be no more death, neither sorrow, nor crying, neither shall there be any more pain: for the former things are passed away."   - Revelation 21:4

The Qur'an's heavenly vision focuses on luxury, leisure and sensual pleasures

Young full-breasted maidens of equal age

"Surely for the god-fearing awaits a place of security, gardens and vineyards and maidens with swelling breasts, like of age, and a cup overflowing"   - Surah 78:31-34
"In both Gardens will be maidens of modest gaze, who no human or jinn has ever touched before"   - Surah 55:56

Sexual pleasures

"They will be reclining on thrones, neatly lined up facing each other. And We will pair them to maidens with gorgeous eyes"
                                    - Surah 78:31-34

Servant boys

"There will circulate among them [servant] boys [especially] for them, as if they were pearls well-protected" - Surah 52:24 | 76:19

Beverage | wine

"They shall be given to drink a pure and delightfully refreshing beverage | wine sealed (and secure from all contamination)"

- Surah 83:25

"Here is the parable of Paradise which the God-fearing have been promised: in it shall be rivers of incorruptible water, rivers of milk unchanging in taste, and rivers of wine, a delight to those that drink.."   - Surah 47:15

The Market Of Paradise

In Paradise there is a street to which they would come every Friday. The north wind will blow and would scatter fragrance on their faces and on their clothes and would add to their beauty and loveliness, and then they would go back to their family after having an added lustre to their beauty and loveliness, and their family would say to them: By Allah, you have been increased in beauty and loveliness after leaving us, and they would say: By Allah, you have also increased in beauty and loveliness after us.

Reference: Sahih Muslim 2833

In-book reference: Book 53, Hadith 15

Food they desire

"And the meat of fowl, from whatever they desire"
                                            - Surah 56:21
"And We will continually provide them with whatever fruit or meat they desire"
                                            - Surah 52:22

Attitude towards others in Bible

"Love the Lord your God with all your heart and with all your soul and with all your mind and with all your strength. The second is this: **'Love your neighbor as yourself.'** There is no commandment greater than these."
                                            - Mark 12:30,31

Attitude towards others in Quran

"Muhammad is the Messenger of Allah. And those who are with him are **hard against the disbelievers**, tender among themselves..."
                                            - Surah 48:29
"O believers! **Fight the disbelievers** around you and **let them find firmness** in you. And know that Allah is with those mindful of Him."
                                            - Surah 9:123

"Now for the matters you wrote about: It is good for a man not to marry. But since there is so much immorality, each man should have his own wife, and each woman her own husband. The **husband should fulfill his marital duty to his wife, and likewise the wife to her husband**. The wife's body does not belong to her alone but also to her husband. **In the same way, the husband's body does not belong to him alone but also to his wife**. Do not deprive each other except by **mutual consent** and for a time, so that you may devote yourselves to prayer. Then come together again so that Satan will not tempt you because of your lack of self-control."
- 1 Corinthians 7:1-5

"Husbands, in the same way be considerate as you live with your wives, and treat them with respect as the weaker partner and as **heirs with you of the gracious gift of life**, so that nothing will hinder your prayers."
- 1 Peter 3:7

"Husbands, **love your wives, just as Christ loved the church** and gave himself up for her to make her holy, cleansing her by the washing with water through the word, and to present her to himself as a radiant church, without stain or wrinkle or any other blemish, but holy and blameless. In this same way, **husbands ought to love their wives as their own bodies**. He who loves his wife loves himself. After all, no one ever hated his own body, but he feeds and cares for it, just as Christ does the church - for we are members of his body. 'For this reason a man will leave his father and mother and be united to his wife, and the two will become one flesh.' This is a profound mystery - but I am talking about Christ and the church. However, each one of you also must love his wife as he loves himself, and the wife must respect her husband."   - Ephesians 5:25-33

"Husbands, love your wives and **do not be harsh** with them."   -Colossians 3:19

"Fair in the eyes of men is the **love of things they covet: women** and sons; Heaped-up hoards of gold and silver; horses branded (for blood and excellence); and (wealth of) cattle and **well-tilled land. Such are the possessions of this world's life**; but with Allah is the best of the goals (to return to)."

— Surah 3:14

"Men are superior to women on account of the qualities which God hath gifted the one above the other, and on account of the outlay they make from their substance for them. Virtuous women are obedient, careful, during the husband's absence, because God hath of them been careful. But chide those for whose refractoriness ye have cause to fear; remove them into beds apart, **and scourge them**: but if they are obedient to you then seek not occasion against them: verily, God is High, Great!"

— Surah 4:34

"**Your wives are as a tilth unto you; so approach your tilth when or how ye will**; but do some good act for your souls beforehand; and fear Allah. And know that ye are to meet Him (in the Hereafter), and give (these) good tidings to those who believe." - Surah 2:223

These are only few references about treating women | wife. There are plenty of references from Quran as well as Hadith which shows how pathetic is Allah's view (Muhammad's view) on women (even towards baby girls). We will be working on this subject alone in our next book deeply.

Setting- and Rising Place of the Sun

Until, when he reached the setting of the sun, he found it [as if] **setting in a spring of dark mud**, and he found near it a people. Allah said, "O Dhul-Qarnayn, either you punish [them] or else adopt among them [a way of] goodness."   - Surah 18:86

"Until, when he came to the rising of the sun, he found it rising on a people for whom We had not made against it any shield"
                                        - Surah 18:90

Stars are there to throw at Devils

"And We have certainly beautified the nearest heaven with **stars and have made [from] them what is thrown at the devils** and have prepared for them the punishment of the Blaze"   - Surah 67:5

Moon is farther than stars

"Do you not consider how **Allah has created seven heavens in layers**. And **made the moon a light in their midst**, and made the sun as a (Glorious) Lamp?"   - Surah 71: 15,16
"Indeed, We have adorned the **nearest heaven with an adornment of stars**"
                                        - Surah 37:6

Sperm originating between the backbone and ribs

"He is created from a drop emitted-Proceeding from between the **backbone and the ribs**"   - Surah 86:6,7

Humans created from a clot of blood

"..then placed each human as a sperm-drop in a secure place, then We developed the **drop into a clinging clot of blood**, then developed the **clot into a lump of flesh**, then developed the **lump into bones**, then **clothed the bones with flesh**, then We brought it into being as a new creation. So Blessed is Allah, the Best of Creators."   - Surah 23:13,14

"And Allah has made the earth for you **as a carpet (spread out)**"   - Surah 71:19
"As for the earth, We **spread it out** and placed upon it firm mountains, and caused everything to grow there in perfect balance."
                - Surah 15:19
"And He will leave the earth **a level plain**"
                - Surah 20:106

"And **He has cast into the earth firmly set mountains, lest it shift with you**, and [made] rivers and roads, that you may be guided,"
                - Surah 16:15
"Have We not **spread the earth like a bed, and fixed the mountains like pegs,**"
                - Surah 78:6,7

The scope of this booklet doesn't allow us to include all the errors in Quran. Apart from that, if we go to Hadith, there are plenty of blunders which alone can be the subject of a book. For example -

Dipping flies into drinks

"The Prophet said "**If a house fly falls in the drink** of anyone of you, **he should dip it (in the drink)**, for one of its wings has a disease and the other has the cure for the disease."
- Sahih Bukhari 4:54:537

CONCLUSION

As it is a quick reference booklet, we are concluding here. We hope that you are able to learn that Islam at it's core is entirely different from Christianity. Do not trap into the deception. Let the truth set you free.

"Who is the liar, if it is not the one who denies that Jesus is the Christ? **This is the antichrist, who denies the Father and the Son.**"
- 1 John 2:22

"Then you will know the truth, and the truth will set you free"
- John 8:32
Jesus answered, "I am the way and the truth and the life. No one comes to the Father except through me."
- John 14:6

FACTON

FACTON is an initiative focused on empowering Christians using various media. We analyze and expose social movements and religions in the light of God's word and thus help the believers to keep themselves from the deception of this world.